Toys and Treasures

How to Open a Successful Collectibles Business

Table of Contents

Chapter 1. Introduction

Welcome to our Special Report, "Toys and Treasures: How to Open a Successful Collectibles Business"! This comprehensive guide is brimming with valuable information on unleashing your entrepreneurial passion in the enticing world of collectibles. From iconic toys to treasured memorabilia, our report offers an enchanting journey into creating a business model that inspires and thrives. It's time to turn your affection for collectibles into a successful enterprise! Exciting insights, vital tips and proven strategies all bundled together to help your venture carve a niche, right at your fingertips. Ready to let the magic begin? Grab your copy of the special report today and embark on an incredible journey of creating your successful, smile-inducing business, one collectible at a time. Lasting success is just a treasure-trove away!

Chapter 2. Exploring the Journey: Understanding the Collectibles Market

The world of collectibles is much more than a simple array of items ranging from toys, stamps, coins, to sports memorabilia. It's a vibrant and often competitive market, interspersed with passionate collectors, hobbyists, and entrepreneurs keen on finding treasures from nostalgia or rarity. To attain success in the collectibles business, a deep understanding of the market is quintessential. This chapter will take you through a comprehensive exploration of the collectibles market, focusing on market dynamics, key value factors, the impact of technology, and more.

2.1. Understanding Collectibles and the Value Proposition

Each piece of collectible, whether it's a vintage toy, a rare baseball card, or a mint condition comic book, carries an inherent value beyond its material worth. This value can be emotional, historical, or related to the item's rarity. Unravelling these value propositions is critical to understanding the market and being successful in it. Nostalgia, for instance, has driven the values of iconic toys from the 80s and 90s through the roof, as collectors seek tangible connections to their childhoods.

Value can also be influenced by cultural or historical significance. Look at the domain of rare books, where a first edition of a classic novel can fetch eye-watering prices. The same holds true for movie memorabilia, sports collectibles, and vintage fashion pieces.

2.2. The Dynamics of the Collectibles Market

The collectibles market can be seen as a dynamic ecosystem where supply, demand, and pricing are in a constant state of flux. Understanding these dynamics can help a business navigate the twists and turns of the market.

Collectibles are typically a scarce commodity, and their rarity is what often forms the cornerstone of their value. This scarcity can be inherent, as with found artifacts, or intentionally created, as with limited edition releases. As the business owner, understanding where your products fit into the supply chain can be a key to your success.

Demand can, at times, be unpredictable, especially given the emotional and subjective nature of the collecting hobby. Factors such as societal trends, individual passion, release of related media content, and even celebrity endorsements can impact demand. Being responsive to these changes can keep your business at the forefront of the market.

Lastly, pricing can be a challenging aspect to manage. Unlike traditional goods, collectibles' pricing can't be easily standardized because of the variability in their value factors - condition, rarity, demand, etc. Developing a pricing strategy that caters to both the emotional and financial investment of your customers is crucial.

2.3. Profits and Challenges

While the collectibles business can be profitable, with items often appreciating over time, one must also factor in risks and potential challenges. The market can be unpredictable, the cost of acquiring and storing the collectibles can be high, and counterfeit goods can pose serious threats. A successful business will have strategies in place to mitigate these risks.

2.4. Impact of Technology

Advancements in technology have reshaped the collectibles market. Online marketplaces, auction sites, and social media platforms have made it easier for buyers and sellers to connect, transact, and share knowledge. They also offer opportunities to reach global markets, and in some instances, have encouraged the rise in value of certain collectibles.

However, the advent of technology also brings challenges such as counterfeit or replica items being sold as originals. Effective use of technology can help businesses grow, but they must also navigate these potential pitfalls to protect their reputation and their customers.

2.5. Exploring the Market Segments

Understanding who your customers are, what drives them, and what they're willing to pay can give you the edge over competitors. The collectibles market isn't a single entity but a combination of many different segments, each with its unique characteristics. Whether your customers are motivated by nostalgia, investing, or the thrill of the hunt, tailoring your service to meet their specific needs can make your business stand out.

In conclusion, the path to success in the collectibles business involves a deep dive into understanding the market, its dynamics, its participants, and the influential role of technology. With this knowledge, your business can carve a niche, stand out, and thrive in this exciting world of treasured collectibles. Remember, every journey starts with a single step, and this understanding provides the first strides on your adventure in the collectibles business.

Chapter 3. Tales to Remember: Iconic Toys and their Historical Significance

For many, toys are not just objects of play; they are nostalgic pieces that carry stories of our childhoods, our societies, even our human history. No matter the generation, one can point to a classic toy and remember the joy it brought. In the collectibles business, understanding the historical significance of iconic toys can greatly boost your commerce by connecting with customers on a deeper emotional level.

3.1. The World Before Plastic: Antique Toys

The history of toys is as old as human civilization itself. In ancient societies, children played with dolls made from materials such as clay and wood, while boys in ancient Greece and Rome played with yo-yos made of wood or metal.

In the 18th and 19th centuries, toys became more elaborate with the introduction of mechanization. For instance, Germany produced intricate tin toys such as trains, horses, and carriages that were sought after worldwide. These toys, viewed as antiques today, fetch impressive prices at auctions because they are not only exceptional pieces of artistry but also capture the essence of a bygone era when every toy was painstakingly handcrafted.

Toys from this era also provide insights into societal norms and values. Paper dolls with elaborate wardrobes, sawdust-filled Raggedy Ann dolls, and tin soldiers were created to prepare children for their future roles in society. Today, these vintage toys form an integral part of many a collection, cherished for their historical significance and the glance they offer into the past.

3.2. The Twentieth Century: Golden Age of Toys

The 20th century revolutionized the toy industry. With the advent of mass production, chemically synthesized material like plastic, and electricity, toys became more affordable and widespread. Teddy bears, Barbie dolls, Lego bricks - these icons of the century not only became a part of playrooms but also cultural phenomena.

The Teddy bear, based on a political cartoon featuring President Theodore Roosevelt, has a place in almost every child's heart. Its creation story, mirroring historical events, adds to its allure and it's now an item rich in nostalgia.

Likewise, Barbie, introduced in 1959, became an instant success. With her changing professions and lifestyles, Barbie mirrored societal changes, women's empowerment, fashion evolution, and more. She became more than just a doll - an inspiration and sometimes a source of controversy.

Lego, on the other hand, brought a new dimension to play. With its 'system of play,' Lego fostered creativity, making each child a 'builder.' Over the years, the Lego Group not only extended its range but also collaborated with popular franchises, turning their bricks into highly collectible items.

3.3. Modern Era: The Dawn of Licensed Merchandises

As television and movies became central to pop culture in the late 20th century, toy companies began to realize the potential of licensed merchandise. The late 1970s and early 1980s opened the door to what would become one of the most successful marketing strategies: the mass production of toys based on popular TV shows and movies.

Star Wars, launched in 1977, was the genesis of this trend. The memorabilia, including action figures, models, and lightsabers, sold in droves. These Star Wars collectibles are now treasured possessions, often traded for staggering sums. Not just Star Wars, but other franchises like Harry Potter, Marvel Comics, and Transformers, have all embraced this merchandise model, creating collectibles that weave together story, fantasy, and play.

3.4. Digital Toys and the Future

As we stride further into the 21st century, digital technology is rapidly reshaping the toy industry. While physical toys remain popular, digital toys and games pose a new frontier. Collectibles aren't just physical anymore - take, for instance, NFTs (Non-Fungible Tokens). They substantiate ownership of unique virtual assets, making digital art, virtual real estate, even tweets, collectible.

However, this doesn't mean traditional collectibles are vanishing. On the contrary, the digital space provides new means of trading and auctioning. eBay, for instance, revolutionized the secondary market for collectibles, making it possible to buy a mint-condition Action Man or a rare Strawberry Shortcake doll from halfway around the world.

To conclude, toys are not just fun and games. They're snapshots of history, culture, and societal changes. They evoke a sense of nostalgia and preserve our shared heritage. Whether it be a simple wooden Yo-Yo, a charming Teddy bear, a groundbreaking Lego set, or a modern digital collectible, each carries its tale, its own historical and emotional significance. Understanding these stories can help you carve your niche and connect with customers, ultimately turning your passion for collectibles into a thriving business.

Chapter 4. Scouting Locations: Choosing the Ideal Site for your Store

Starting with the foundation of any profitable brick-and-mortar business - location - let's dive deep into Scout Locations, the heart and soul of a store. A spot with high foot traffic or in a prominent, centralized area could be the difference between a business thriving or merely surviving.

4.1. Understanding Your Business Necessities

Before you start scouting locations, you need to have a clear understanding of your business' requirements. The type of customer you are targeting, the size of the store you need, and your budget will guide your location search process.

You are looking for the best match between your target market and your store location. Is your target customer more likely to shop in a high-end shopping district or a suburban shopping center? You'll need to visualise where your customers live, work and play.

In terms of size, too small a space might limit inventory and make the store congested. Conversely, too large a space might waste valuable resources. But don't just consider immediate needs; plan for future growth as well.

Lastly, your budget is a critical factor. Consider both rent and other associated costs, such as utilities, maintenance, security, and taxes. They all influence affordability.

4.2. The Impact of Surrounding Businesses

Neighboring businesses can significantly impact your introduction to the market. Consider their clientele and product lines. Businesses catering to the same demographic can be beneficial, creating a one-stop-shop environment for customers. On the other hand, direct competition can be challenging. Though if you have a unique selling proposition ready, it could be an opportunity to tap into a pre-existent market.

Check for any businesses around that could potentially drive or distract foot traffic. For instance, a bookstore or a coffee shop might draw in your targeted customers. Conversely, a noise-intensive or industrial-scale company could detract from your shop's ambiance or its easy accessibility.

4.3. Planning for Accessibility

Your store shouldn't be just convenient to reach, but also easy to navigate once inside. Ramps for wheelchair or stroller accessibility and wide lanes for easy movement make for a customer-friendly environment. Increased accessibility solidifies the inclusivity of your brand.

The same consideration extends to parking. Depending on the area and the nature of your business, you might need ample parking space. For urban areas, proximity to public transportation could be crucial. Remember, the easier it is for customers to reach you, the more likely they are to visit.

4.4. Evaluating Foot Traffic

Foot traffic is an important aspect of any retail business. Before settling on a location, visit during different times of the day and week. Observe foot traffic patterns and the demographics of the people who walk by. Today, there are also digital tools available to get data about foot traffic in specific locations.

4.5. Decoding Lease Agreements

When you have a shortlist of potential spots, review lease agreements meticulously. Consult with a real-estate lawyer to understand the lease terms like the duration, renewal options, rent escalation clauses, and tenant and landlord obligations. Mark any clauses that may restrict your store operations, like hours of business operations, signage restrictions, etc.

Also, inquire about your capacity to renovate or remodel the store. Do you have the freedom to adapt the space to your brand's aesthetic and functional needs?

4.6. Future Planning

While considering all of these factors, keep an eye on the future, both yours and the location's. Envision your growth. Will the space accommodate expansion? Can the locality sustain your business as your customer base grows?

Also, review any prospective developments, either pending or planned, in the neighborhood. They might increase or decrease the value or attractiveness of your location.

Finding the right location for your business can be a daunting task. But when done right, it can set the foundation for your business's long-term success. A great location will not just enhance your store's visibility but also influence the kind of clientele you attract. It can vastly impact your foot traffic, and ultimately, your bottom line. So, take your time to evaluate, plan and pick the perfect spot for your dream collectible store.

Chapter 5. The Nitty-Gritty: Business Plan and Legal Considerations

Starting a new venture in the world of collectibles is indeed an exciting journey, but it's not all about procuring and selling charming pieces - there's a nitty-gritty aspect that must be covered meticulously. Understanding this aspect is paramount to creating a solid foundation for your business. This chapter encompasses an in-depth exploration of creating a robust business plan and understanding your legal obligations to navigate your entrepreneurial journey seamlessly.

5.1. Crafting a Robust Business Plan

An efficacious business plan serves as a roadmap for your venture, outlining the course of action for the growth and stability of your business. Let's delve into the components of this indispensable tool.

5.1.1. Executive Summary

The executive summary is an overview of your business plan. It should be compelling enough to engage your audience's attention. This section includes your business name, location, and a succinct description of the product or service your company provides. Also, showcase your unique selling propositions and briefly introduce your leadership team.

5.1.2. Business Description

Here, provide detailed information about your collectibles business, the problem that your company will solve, and how it will stand apart from competitors. Include information about the niche you target, the market's size, and your anticipated position in it. Categorize your products, discussing their uniqueness and appeal.

5.1.3. Market Analysis

Market analysis gives you insights into your industry, market, and competitors. This analysis comprises market needs, market trends, and a competitive analysis. Detailed research on the size, demographics, consumer behavior, and growth rate of your target market can define your selling and marketing strategies.

5.1.4. Organization and Management

Outline your business structure and the profiles of your management team. Provide an organizational chart, detailing each team member's responsibilities. Highlight their skills, educational background, prior work experience, and notable achievements.

5.1.5. Services or Product Line

Here, describe your collectibles and the appeal they offer to your customers. Discuss the pricing, lifespan, and your product sourcing strategy. If you have patents or copyrights, mention them here.

5.1.6. Marketing and Sales

Your marketing and sales strategy is the engine that drives your business. Describe your marketing plans, sales strategy, and your customer relationship management programs.

5.1.7. Funding Request

If you're seeking funding from investors, clearly outline your funding requirements, the purpose of the funding, and future financial plans.

5.1.8. Financial Projections

This section includes projected income statements, balance sheets, and cash flow statements for the next 3-5 years. Include an analysis with a break-even point that indicates when your business will be profitable.

5.1.9. Exit Strategy

An exit strategy anticipates the endgame of your business. This could be in the form of a merger, an acquisition, or even a public offering.

5.2. Legal Considerations

When entering the world of collectibles, it's essential to understand the legal facets to ensure your business operates within the bounds of law.

5.2.1. Business Structure

Define your business structure. Options include sole proprietorship, partnership, Limited Liability Company (LLC), or a corporation. Each structure involves different tax obligations, liability concerns, and administrative tasks, so choose wisely.

5.2.2. Licensing and Permits

Depending upon your location, you may require certain licenses and permits to operate your collectibles business. Enlist professional help to understand the requisite documents and adhere strictly to the guidelines to avoid legal issues.

5.2.3. Insurance

Business insurance secures your investment by minimizing financial risks associated with unexpected events like an injury, death, or lawsuit. Some insurance specifically tailored for collectibles businesses includes product liability insurance and business interruption insurance. Consult with an insurance advisor to identify your business's potential risks.

5.2.4. Taxes

Understanding your tax obligations is crucial as a business owner. Depending on your business structure, you may need to pay self-employment tax, federal income tax, state income tax, or sales tax. Hire a competent accountant to ensure you're meeting all your tax responsibilities.

5.2.5. Legal Challenges

Several legal challenges are peculiar to the collectibles business, such as ownership rights, copyright infringement, and authentication issues. Acquaint yourself with these issues and consider seeking professional legal advice.

Building a successful business is a meticulous process that requires careful planning and adherence to legal norms. Hopefully, this chapter provided you with valuable insights into crafting a sound business plan and understanding your legal obligations in starting your collectibles venture. With this understanding, you are well on your way to turning your passion into a rewarding and successful business.

Remember, passion is essential in the collectibles business, but good planning and legal acumen are crucial for long-term success. Maintain a balance of these elements, and you'll find your path in the collectibles industry paved with success.

Chapter 6. Building Connections: Leveraging Suppliers and Industry Networks

As you embark on the fantastic journey of creating a successful collectibles business, building solid connections with suppliers, industry networks, and other related businesses is pivotal to your success. A strong, supportive network can help drive your business to dizzying heights of success.

6.1. Developing Relationships with Suppliers

A successful collectibles business is heavily dependent on a continuous supply of commodities that cater to various tastes and investments. Thus, finding and sustaining relationships with competent suppliers is a critical step.

Begin by identifying potential suppliers. Attend trade shows, scour online platforms, or use directories to find suppliers dealing in your niche of collectibles. Once you've identified potential suppliers, reach out to them. Express your business intentions and requirements. Clear communication is key in developing and maintaining relationships.

Remember, suppliers aren't just sources for your products; they're sources for industry knowledge and contacts. Regular, clear communication — via meetings, phone calls, emails — can foster this partnership. Keep them informed about your business plans, discuss market trends, and always ask for their inputs. Their business experiences can provide you with valuable insights and market forecasts.

Negotiation is another crucial aspect of dealing with suppliers. Always bargain on more than just the price — consider delivery times, payment terms, and purchase quantities. Building a flexible and mutually beneficial relationship will further strengthen your ties.

Remember to always have a backup supplier at hand. Unforeseen circumstances may arise – a supplier may go out of business, or there might be shipping issues. Having one or more backup suppliers ensures your business remains operational and flexible to changes in situation.

6.2. Cultivating Industry Networks

While suppliers provide the lifeblood for your business, industry networks form the support structure. Experts, peers, and influencers can provide advice, endorsements, and customer referrals. They can also aid in fostering a sense of belonging in the industry.

Online platforms and forums provide excellent opportunities to connect with collectors and enthusiasts alike. These platforms often host discussions about market trends, popular collectibles and valuable tips shared by industry veterans. These interactions can help refine your business strategies, based on insights directly from your target audience and industry peers.

Attending trade shows, conventions, and auctions can also provide networking opportunities. They allow face-to-face interactions that often lead to deeper, more personal relationships. Furthermore, attending such events can showcase your dedication and passion for the field, positioning you as a serious player in the market.

Don't overlook the importance of local networks. Joining local business associations and participating in local events can provide distinct advantages. It can put your business on the local map, opening up opportunities for collaborations, partnerships, or even mentorships with established local businesses.

6.3. Engaging with Related Businesses

In addition to suppliers and industry networks, engaging with businesses related to your field can be immensely beneficial. These might include packaging companies, logistics providers, or even local businesses that complement your offerings. For example, a vintage toy collectible store can form beneficial partnerships with a local comic book shop.

These partnerships can help you tap into new customer bases, cross-promote products, or negotiate better deals with service providers. Such relationships can also foster a sense of camaraderie and mutual support often invaluable during tougher business climates.

6.4. Formalizing Relationships

It's vital to document your business relationships for transparency and future reference. Formal agreements including terms, conditions, and roles, provide clarity and protection for all parties involved. While a more informal relationship may suffice in the beginning, as your business grows, the need for formalized relationships increases.

Contracts with suppliers, agreements with business partners, or memorandums of understanding with networks are all examples of formalization. They ensure that all parties involved have a clear understanding of their responsibilities, reducing potential conflicts.

6.5. Enduring Relationships through Troubled Times

Business landscapes are ever changing, often troubled by uncertainties and unexpected challenges. In such circumstances, the strength of your business connections can play a defining role in the durability of your enterprise. It's during these trying times that the value of fostering solid relationships truly shine.

Support each other through challenges, be patient with temporary difficulties, and collaborate to find solutions together. Such bonds not only strengthen your business but also contribute positively to the entire industry ecosystem.

In summary, establishing and nurturing robust connections with suppliers, industry networks, and related businesses is quintessential for running a successful collectibles business. These potent connections not only provide a stable business operating system but also enrich you with crucial market insights, beneficial collaborations, and enduring industry relationships. With solid networks in place, you're well-equipped to navigate the exhilarating world of collectibles, marking your path to a thriving and fruitful business.

Chapter 7. Priceless or Worthless? Learning to Appraise Collectibles

Before stepping into the world of collectibles, knowing how to discern the priceless from the worthless is a crucial skill that can shape your business's fortune. Many collectibles have hidden value, and unlocking it requires a keen eye and an understanding of the market. Fortunately, much of this can be learned and developed, enriching the experience of dealing with collectibles and making commerce more appealing and profitable.

7.1. Understanding the Market Value

Understanding the market value of a collectible is fundamental. It requires a good grasp of buyer preferences, current trends, and historical selling prices. Various factors contribute to an item's value—age, rarity, condition, and even cultural significance.

An excellent starting point is online platforms and auctions sites where similar items have been sold. Sites such as eBay or Sotheby's provide comprehensive databases of past sales. Comprehensive guides, like the Overstreet Comic Book Price Guide for comic book collections, can also be helpful.

7.2. Rarity and Scarcity

One of the primary factors impacting the value of a collectible is how rare or scarce it is. The basic principle of supply and demand—and the fact that fewer items mean higher demand—effectively increases the value of infrequent collectibles. Determining rarity may involve research into how many of those items were produced and how many are currently in circulation.

======= The Role of Condition

The condition of a collectible is paramount. The better preserved it is, the higher the value. Various grading systems are applied depending on the type of collectible. For instance, coin grading ranges from Poor (P-1) to Perfect Mint State (MS-70). Understanding these grading standards is essential, and professional grading services can be a reliable resource in assessing a collectible's condition.

For items such as dolls, action figures, and toys, being in an unopened box or having untampered original packaging significantly increases value.

7.3. Authenticity Verification

Authenticity is paramount when valuing collectibles. Few things can devalue an item more quickly than questions about its authenticity. Understanding how to verify authenticity, whether through distinguishing marks, serial numbers, or validated certificates, can differentiate between making a profit and suffering a loss.

7.4. Historical, Cultural, and Sentimental Value

These factors add a less tangible, but equally important dimension to a collectible's value. For instance, sports memorabilia linked with a significant event or a famous personality can have high value due to its historic or cultural importance. Similarly, items from a popular film or cult classic can fetch high prices due to their sentimental value to fans.

7.5. The Appraisal Process

An appraisal is a formal, impartial judgment or estimate of a collectible's value. It is conducted by professionals who specialize in the type of collectible you own. If you own a collectible item of significant value or are not confident in your ability to appraise it accurately, hiring a professional appraiser is highly recommended.

To find professional appraisers, you may check databases like the American Society of Appraisers (ASA) or the Appraisers Association of America.

7.6. Appraising Online

Virtual appraisal services have gained popularity in recent times. They are more accessible, often cheaper, and can be just as reliable as in-person services. Websites like ValueMyStuff and WorthPoint can offer online appraisals.

Remember to weigh the costs of an appraisal against the potential added value of the item. An appraisal might not be worthwhile if it doesn't significantly increase the item's value.

7.7. Final Words

Becoming knowledgeable in appraising your collectibles will not only save you money but also prevent you from falling for deceitful tactics. It also allows you to be the final arbiter over the items you decide to add to your collection or sell in your business. As you become more comfortable identifying markers of worth and value, you'll also become more adept at determining what you should pay for them.

Remember, appraisals are part science, part art form, relying on solid research, expert opinions, and at times a little gut instinct. With patience and practice, your skills in appraising collectibles will surely grow, assisting you in building a successful collectibles business.

Chapter 8. Keeping it Fresh: Sourcing and Rotating Your Inventory

Az successful collectibles business thrives on the variety and freshness of the inventory. Knowing where to source your products and how often to rotate them is crucial, as it will keep your customers engaged and coming back for more.

8.1. Sourcing your Inventory

Let's start by discussing where to source your collectibles from. There are many places to discover unique items, all varying in reliability, cost, and rarity of the items you can find.

One: Auctions and Estate Sales

Auctions and estate sales can be a valuable source of fresh inventory. These sales often include vast collections of items, some of which might be extremely rare. Research upcoming auctions and sales in your local area, as well as online platforms that host these events.

Two: Online Marketplaces:

Online marketplaces like eBay, Craigslist, and Etsy are bustling with a diverse range of collectibles. Drawing from these sources requires a keen eye for value and an understanding of what your customers desire. Consistently monitor these platforms for new listings.

Three: Wholesale Suppliers:

Consider partnering with wholesale suppliers who deal in collectibles. While this may require a significant initial investment, it guarantees a steady supply of popular items. Remember, the essence of a fruitful partnership with these suppliers is a healthy interaction where mutual needs are addressed.

Four: Yard or Garage Sales:

Yard or garage sales often have unique items at low prices. Local sales often require legwork to attend and research, but the low cost of items can result in a higher profit margin.

Five: Direct from Creators:

Sourcing items directly from creators can be a unique way to stock one-of-a-kind pieces. This method is particularly effective if you're dealing in contemporary collectibles. It allows you to form a personal relationship with the artist, understand their work, and convey their story to your customers.

8.2. Evaluating Potential Inventory

Now that you know where to source your collectibles, it's essential to understand how to evaluate any potential items. There are several key points to consider:

One: Authenticity of the Collectibles:

Make sure to verify the authenticity of any collectible you consider purchasing. Fake or counterfeit items can damage your reputation and harm your business. Learn about the specific makers' marks, serial numbers, or characteristics that can authenticate an item.

Two: Condition of the Collectibles:

The condition of a collectible significantly influences its value. Items in mint or near-mint condition will yield a higher value than those with visible damage or wear. Educate yourself about grading scales for various types of collectibles, and factor in restoration costs for any damaged items.

Three: Profitability:

Always consider the potential resale value of an item. You should be able to sell it for a profit after deducting all costs associated with procuring and maintaining it. Research the marketplace, understand what drives demand, and identify profitable trends.

8.3. Rotating your Inventory

Remember, your customers are excited by novelty. Therefore, regularly reinvigorating your inventory is a necessity. There are a few strategies you should employ to keep things fresh:

One: Seasonal Rotation:

Align your inventory with the seasons or holidays. This approach can apply to all sorts of collectibles. In the lead-up to Christmas, for example, vintage ornaments or toys from holiday-themed TV shows will be particularly appealing to customers.

Two: Spotting Trends:

Stay ahead of trends. Monitor pop culture closely and stock up on items related to popular franchises, television shows, movies, or celebrities. As interest rises, these items will be in high demand.

Three: Creating Variety:

Even within your niche, variety matters. If you are selling vintage toys, for example, offer items from a range of different periods and manufacturers. This broad spectrum of products will appeal to a wider range of customers and keep them engaged with your business.

Four: Regular Inventory Updates:

Promote your regular updates to inventory through an email

newsletter or social media channels. It will help cultivate a sense of anticipation and excitement among your customers. Moreover, it can be a great way to draw attention to new or particularly interesting items in your stock.

8.4. Maintaining your Inventory

Finally, maintaining your inventory in good shape is essential. Consider investing in display cases, protective sheets, and other materials that prevent damage. Additionally, regular cleaning and dusting can keep your items in peak condition. Depending on the nature of your collectibles, it might also be necessary to control environmental factors like light, temperature, and humidity.

Your inventory is the lifeblood of your collectibles business. Sourcing unique items, ensuring their authenticity and condition, regularly rotating your stock, and maintaining the items in your care will help you craft an appealing experience for your customers. With careful attention to these areas, you can create and sustain a thriving business in the warm, nostalgic glow of collectibles.

Chapter 9. Creating the Sparkle: Marketing and Promotions in the Collectibles World

The prospect of opening a successful collectibles business is enticing but thriving in the competitive landscape calls for strategic marketing and promotions. This isn't merely about announcing your presence, but crafting a tale that entices, intricates resonating with the emotions of your target audience, and thereby fostering a community around your collectibles.

9.1. Understanding Your Target Market

To create an effective marketing strategy, deep comprehending of your target market is paramount. Collectibles cater to a wide variety of people, but not every demographic or psychographic will be interested in your products. For instance, vintage toy collectors may not have an interest in sports memorabilia and vice versa. Thus, identifying your primary customer base is the first step towards creating a persuasive and impactful narrative around your collectibles.

Use demographics like age, location, income level and psychographics like hobbies, interests, and lifestyles to refine your target audience. With this understanding, create buyer personas - semi-fictional characters that represent your ideal customers. These personas help to warp your strategies in the customer's perspective, letting you design more relevant and persuasive campaigns.

9.2. Crafting a Unique Selling Proposition

The Unique Selling Proposition (USP) separates your collectibles business from the competition. It's not just about what you offer but how you offer products that matter. A captivating USP could be your range of rare items, unique packaging, customized delivery, customer service, or the shopping experience.

Try to think about what makes your business stand out. Highlighting this differentiation in your marketing efforts will help draw attention and intrigue your potential consumers.

9.3. Influencer Collaborations and Partnerships

In the age of social media, influencers, with their substantial followers, can be a potent tool to reach your target audience. Find influencers who share the same passions as your brand, request them to promote your collectibles. Remember, the influencer's audience demographics should align with your target market. A sports memorabilia shop collaborating with a popular sports blogger or athlete, for instance, can pave the way for effective engagement.

Partnerships with complementary businesses can also amplify your reach. Comic book stores, hobby shops, or pop culture conventions can be great avenues for collaboration.

9.4. Capitalize on Content Marketing

Content is king in the modern marketing landscape. Share captivating stories about your collectibles, the history behind vintage items, or showcase exclusive pieces. Use the power of visual content such as photographs, infographics, and videos to engage the audience and evoke a sense of longing.

Utilize blogs or social media platforms to share this content. Additionally, consider launching a YouTube channel or podcast to delve deeper into the world of collectibles. This educative, engaging content will not only draw customers but also position your brand as an authority in collectible items.

9.5. Leverage Special Occasions and Mega Events

Release limited-edition items or offer discounts during occasions such as holidays or blockbuster movie releases. Create a sense of urgency to boost sales.

Mega events like comic cons, toy fairs, or sports tournaments are golden opportunities to showcase your offerings. Engage with the community, host events, involve in sponsorships or create pop-up shops to lure collectors.

9.6. SEO and Digital Advertising

Harnessing the power of SEO and digital advertising is fundamental to reach millions within microseconds. Incorporate keywords into your website content that potential customers might use to search for collectibles. Regularly update your website and optimize it for mobile devices.

Leverage Google ads, sponsored social media posts, or PPC (Pay-Per-Click) ads to amplify your business reach. Retargeting ads towards people who've visited your website but didn't make a purchase would also help to improve sales.

9.7. Customer Satisfaction and Loyalty Programs

Remember, a satisfied customer is your best brand ambassador. Offer superior customer service to help your business flourish in the long-term. Reward regular customers with loyalty programs—offer discounts or exclusive first-view of your limited-edition collectibles to loyal members.

In a nutshell, establishing a strong foothold in the collectibles market requires meticulous planning and customer-centric strategies. The amalgamation of both, classic and modern marketing techniques, catered to your specific audience will give your business the much-needed sparkle. With persistence and creativity, your collectibles business can achieve the allure that invariably translates into success.

Chapter 10. Customer Loyalty: Service Strategies for Repeat Business

In the world of collectibles business, one of the key drivers of success is customer loyalty. Astute entrepreneurs recognize that gaining new customers is just half the battle; the true challenge lies in retaining them. By offering superior service and continually delighting the customer, your business can sustainably fuel repeat business, consistently improve revenue, and rapidly accelerate growth.

10.1. Understanding Customer Loyalty

Let's begin by dissecting the core essence of customer loyalty. In the simplest terms, a loyal customer is one who enjoys your products or services to such an extent that they repeatedly choose your business over your competitors. The loyalty of your customers is the backbone of your business; it is a definitive sign of your triumph in meeting - or exceeding - your customers' expectations.

A loyal customer base is not merely a revenue booster. It is a powerful tool for marketing, a beacon attracting more customers, and a treasury of constructive feedback. Gauging and cultivating customer loyalty requires a fine balance of technical knowledge, strategic foresight, and good old-fashioned people skills.

10.2. Building Customer Loyalty: The Crucial Elements

Several elements play pivotal roles in shaping customer loyalty.

These include product quality, customer service, brand reputation, and overall customer experience. An impeccable blend of these elements gives birth to customer loyalty.

1. Product Quality: The cornerstone of customer loyalty lies in first-rate products. In the collectibles business, product quality spans a myriad of factors - from the integrity of the item to historical significance to the condition in which it is kept. Striving for excelling product quality consistently can be the most unforeseen brand ambassador your business could ask for.

2. Customer Service: The shining star in the pursuit of customer loyalty is undoubtedly top-notch customer service. Ensuring prompt addressal of queries or concerns, providing exhaustive product knowledge, and going the extra mile to make the customer feel valued - these are the hallmarks of exceptional customer service.

3. Brand Reputation: A strong brand reputation is akin to an unstated guarantee for the customers. A reputation for selling genuine, quality collectibles can act as a beacon for collectors and enthusiasts.

4. Customer Experience: Customer experience is the sum of all the touchpoints a customer has with your business. From the ease of browsing your catalogue to the checkout process to post-purchase service, every interaction counts towards customer experience.

10.3. The Power of Exceeding Expectations

The consumer's world is brimming with options. To secure a permanent spot in their hearts and minds, you need to do more than just meet their expectations - you should strive to exceed them. This could mean giving them an exceptionally well-packaged product, providing unexpected bonuses or just a simple 'thank you' note with each purchase to express your gratitude. Adding personal touches and going beyond the call of duty can drive your business to unparalleled levels of customer loyalty.

10.4. Strategies for Instilling Loyalty

Now that we've laid down the necessary foundations, let's delve into the strategies that can help you instill and cultivate customer loyalty.

1. Loyalty Rewards Program: Implementing a loyalty rewards program is a proven way to drive repeat business. Such a program typically rewards customers for repeat purchases or referrals. These rewards could take the form of discounts, exclusive access to new products, or even unique collector's items.

2. Personalized Customer Experience: In the era of digital dominance, personalization is the key to superior customer experience. Utilizing data on customer preferences, purchase history, and feedback can allow businesses to personalize their service.

3. Superior After-Sales Service: After-sales service is often an overlooked factor in customer retention. Offering a flawless service - from shipping and delivery to resolving potential issues promptly and effectively - epitomizes a business that cares for its customers. It invariably results in enhanced customer trust and loyalty.

4. Regular Communication: Regular communication with your customers keeps your business at the forefront of their consciousness. This doesn't mean bombarding them with sales pitches; instead, you could send newsletters about the latest offers, personally wish them on special occasions or share relevant and engaging content about collectibles.

Customer loyalty can indeed be your collectibles business' most potent weapon. Crafting an unmatched shopping experience, providing meticulous service, and endlessly striving for superior value can make your customers your biggest advocates. In the long run, these loyalists will become intrinsic to your business's survival and growth. They will fight off the competition, drive your sales, and above all, provide honest and actionable feedback to keep improving your operations.

Chapter 11. Looking Ahead: Growth and Expansion Possibilities

Starting a collectible business is akin to embarking on a thrilling adventure filled with twists and turns, ups and downs, and an abundance of lessons to learn. However, once you have built a successful foundation, your thoughts must inevitably turn to the prospects for growth and expansion. Horizontal or vertical, local or international, brick-and-mortar or online— the possible directions for expansion are only limited by your ambition and imagination.

11.1. Building a Recognizable Brand

The key to structuring and expanding a successful collectibles business lies in building a brand that resonates with your target audience. This involves defining your unique selling proposition, creating a memorable brand name and logo, and consistently communicating your brand distinctiveness and quality.

- Understand Your Niche: Deepen your understanding of your target market and position your brand accordingly. What do your customers value in a collectibles business? Use this insight to develop a brand image that appeals to them.

- Be Consistent: Branding is about more than just a catchy name or a sleek logo—it's about the consistency of experience. From the quality of your collectibles to your customer service, each touchpoint with your customers is an opportunity to reinforce your brand.

Once your brand has gained traction and recognition, you can leverage this goodwill to enter new markets or introduce new products.

11.2. Expanding Your Range

Diversification can be an excellent strategy for growth. By extending your range of products, you can capture a broader market, reduce the risk of dependence on a single category, and potentially increase your sales and profitability.

- Research the Market: Identify categories of collectibles that have a high demand and potential for profit. Use customer suggestions, track buying trends, and observe what's selling in other markets.

- Understand the Logistics: Each category of collectibles will have its logistics and considerations. Through careful planning and preparation, understand how each new category will impact your sourcing, storage, and delivery.

Remember, the key to effective diversification is to start small, test, learn and adapt.

11.3. Going Online

If your business does not have an online presence yet, then establishing one could be your next big step. An online presence can help you reach more customers, particularly those outside your local area.

- Build a User-friendly Website: Your website is your digital storefront. Make it user-friendly, optimized for search engines, and rich with valuable content.

- Leverage Social Media: Platforms like Instagram, Facebook, Pinterest can help you connect directly with your audience, showcase your offerings, and build a community around your brand.

11.4. Cross-border Expansion

Expanding your business across borders can bring more opportunities, but it also exposes you to new challenges and risks: different customer preferences, tougher competition, unfamiliar regulations, and more.

- Understand the Market: Do comprehensive research to understand potential markets' culture, consumer behavior, competition, and governmental regulations about collectibles.

- Build Local Partnerships: Partnerships with local businesses can help you navigate the complexities of a new market. They can provide insights, advice, and resources that may be otherwise inaccessible.

The path to growth and expansion can be arduous and fraught with obstacles. But with careful planning, a persistent spirit, and the tips in this guide, you can turn your collectibles business into a thriving enterprise. Remember, every step should be measured, deliberate, and calculated. As they say, "Rome wasn't built in a day". Good luck with your journey, and may your business prosper beyond your wildest dreams.

www.ingramcontent.com/pod-product-compliance
Lightning Source LLC
Chambersburg PA
CBHW060854260726
48661CB00008B/3253